# SOCCER CHAMPIONS

**BY JIM WHITING**

# RIVER PLATE

CREATIVE EDUCATION • CREATIVE PAPERBACKS

Published by Creative Education
and Creative Paperbacks
P.O. Box 227, Mankato, Minnesota 56002
Creative Education and Creative Paperbacks
are imprints of The Creative Company
www.thecreativecompany.us

Design by The Design Lab; production by Darrion Hunt
Art direction by Rita Marshall
Printed in China

Photographs by Alamy (Chronicle, Jonathan Gordon,
StampsCorner, World History Archive), Creative Commons
Wikimedia (Amarhgil, Argentine Football Association
Library, *Clarín*, General Archive of the Nation, *El Gráfico*,
Moebiusuibeom-en, oliveraclaudio, La Página Millonaria,
Revista Estadio/Biblioteca Nacional Digital de Chile,
Unknown), Getty Images (Chris Brunskill Ltd/Getty Images
Sport, Marcelo Endelli/Stringer/LatinContent WO, Daniel
Jayo/LatinContent WO, Keystone/Hulton Archive, JUAN
MABROMATA/AFP, Amilcar Orfali/LatinContent WO,
Gabriel Rossi/LatinContent WO), Newscom (NICOLAS
AGUILERA/EFE, TELAM Xinhua News Agency, Wolfgang
Weihs/picture-alliance/dpa, Martin Zabala/Xinhua
News Agency), Shutterstock (gualtiero boffi, R-O-M-A)

Library of Congress Cataloging-in-Publication Data
Names: Whiting, Jim, author.
Title: River Plate / Jim Whiting.
Series: Soccer champions.
Includes bibliographical references and index.
Summary: A chronicle of the people, matches,
and world events that shaped the South American
men's Argentine soccer team known as River
Plate, from its founding in 1901 to today.
Identifiers: LCCN 2017059837
ISBN 978-1-60818-978-6 (hardcover)
ISBN 978-1-62832-605-5 (pbk)
ISBN 978-1-64000-079-7 (eBook)
Subjects: LCSH: 1. River Plate (Athletic club)—
History—Juvenile literature. 2. Soccer players—
Argentina—Biography—Juvenile literature.

Classification: LCC GV943.6.R53 W55
20185 / DDC 796.3340982—dc23

CCSS: RI.5.1, 2, 3, 8; RH.6-8.4, 5, 7

First Edition HC 9 8 7 6 5 4 3 2 1
First Edition PBK 9 8 7 6 5 4 3 2 1

Cover and page 3: Midfielder Leonardo Ponzio
Page 1: 2016 Copa Libertadores

TABLE OF

# CONTENTS

Defender Germán Pezzella

# INTRODUCTION

Soccer (or football, as it is known almost everywhere outside of the United States) is truly a universal game. Originating in Europe, it quickly spread to the rest of the world. The Fédération Internationale de Football Association (FIFA), the international governing body of soccer, is divided into six confederations. The Confederación Sudamericana de Fútbol (CONMEBOL) regulates soccer in South America. Nearly every country has at least one league with several divisions. At the end of each season, the bottommost teams in one division are relegated (moved down) to the next lower division, while the same number of topmost teams from that lower division move up to replace them. This ensures a consistently high level of competition. Late-season games between teams with losing records still feature spirited competition as both sides seek to avoid relegation.

Founded as the Argentine Association Football League (AAFL) in 1893, the renamed Asociación del Fútbol Argentino (AFA) organizes leagues in Argentina. The season concludes with a champion determined by points gained throughout the season. Teams receive three points for a win and one point for a tie. The top league in Argentina is the Superliga Argentina. Long known as the Primera División, it has undergone a number of format

*As of 2017, River Plate had won more Primera División/Superliga titles than any other team.*

changes during its history. Some of these changes resulted in two separate competitions being held the same year. This created the opportunity for clubs to win two league championships in one year. Currently, the Superliga holds its annual tournament from August to June. It has historically been dominated by the "Big Five," all of which are based in the Greater Buenos Aires area: River Plate, Boca Juniors, Independiente, Racing Club, and San Lorenzo de Almagro. In recent years, however, other teams have risen to challenge the Big Five.

Another significant championship is the national cup, or Copa Argentina. Originally contested in 1969 and 1970, it was re-established in 2011. Copa Argentina is similar to England's FA Cup or Spain's Copa del Rey. It includes more than 200 teams. The schedule is spread out over nine months, and games are played at neutral sites. The champion takes on the Superliga winner in the Supercopa Argentina.

Continent-wide competitions include Copa Sudamericana, which began in 2002 and now fields up to 50 teams. The Recopa Sudamericana pits the Copa Sudamericana champion against the winner of CONMEBOL's prestigious Copa Libertadores de América. Dating back to 1960, Libertadores is generally regarded as being on a competitive par with Europe's Champions League. It begins with nearly 50 teams and consists of 6 rounds of competition. The winner also plays in the FIFA Club World Cup, an annual seven-team tournament. It includes the top team from each of the six confederations and the host nation. The winner is universally regarded as world champion.

## ALL-TIME COPA LIBERTADORES RECORDS OF THE TOP 11 CLUBS (AS OF 2017):

| | Winner | Runner-up |
|---|---|---|
| Independiente (Argentina) | 7 | 0 |
| Boca Juniors (Argentina) | 6 | 4 |
| Peñarol (Uruguay) | 5 | 5 |
| Estudiantes (Argentina) | 4 | 1 |
| Club Olimpia (Paraguay) | 3 | 4 |
| Nacional (Uruguay) | 3 | 3 |
| São Paulo FC (Brazil) | 3 | 3 |
| Grêmio (Brazil) | 3 | 2 |
| River Plate (Argentina) | 3 | 2 |
| Santos FC (Brazil) | 3 | 1 |
| Cruzeiro (Brazil) | 2 | 2 |

*El Monumental stadium*

# EMBRACING THE ENGLISH GAME

*By around 1900, Buenos Aires had one of the busiest ports in the world.*

By the late 1800s, Argentina had the largest population of English people in any country outside of the British Empire. The English brought their culture to Argentina, including sports such as cricket, polo, rugby, and soccer. The English Football Association's *Laws of the Game* were published in Argentina in 1867. Sixteen Englishmen played the first recorded game of soccer in the country that same year.

By the turn of the century, the AAFL consisted of four divisions. In 1901, two Fourth Division teams—Santa Rosa and La Rosales—decided to merge. The teams

*Many immigrants who arrived in Buenos Aires worked on the docks.*

were located in La Boca, a Buenos Aires neighborhood where the Matanza River flows into the River Plate. The new team needed a name. One of the members, Pedro Martínez, noticed that some dockworkers had taken a break from work to play soccer. The boxes they had been moving were stamped with "The River Plate." English influence in the area was so strong that the new club decided to use "River Plate" for its name rather than the Spanish-language Río de la Plata. Its official name—Club Atlético River Plate—combines both languages.

The team's distinctive uniforms owe their origin to Buenos Aires's Carnival season. During the city's festivities in 1905, two team members saw red ribbons inscribed with "The Inhabitants from Hell" dangling from a float. They ripped off a couple of the ribbons and draped them diagonally across their white shirts to add a touch of color.

With its splash of red, River Plate joined the Third Division. It advanced to the Second Division the following year, where it remained for three seasons. Late in 1908, River defeated Racing Club, which resulted in promotion to the Primera División—or so they thought. Taking note of the disruption caused by jubilant River fans swarming onto the field before the game officially ended, league officials ordered the match to be replayed. River removed any doubt by crushing its opponent 7–0.

River began Primera División play in 1909. To honor

*The 1908 championship club sported the diagonally striped uniforms.*

the promotion, the team replaced the red slash with vertical white, red, and black stripes, which it would continue wearing until 1932. The highlight of that inaugural Primera season was a 1–0 victory over Alumni, Argentina's dominant team at the beginning of the 20th century. It was Alumni's only loss that season. The team's low point was a 10–1 thumping at the hands of Club Atlético Belgrano. Despite that humiliating defeat, River finished second in the division.

In 1914, River won its first significant titles. The team crushed Newell's Old Boys in the final of the countrywide Copa de Competencia Jockey Club tournament. That qualified River for the Copa de Competencia Chevallier Boutell. Commonly known as the Tie Cup, the game set the winner of the Jockey Club against the champion of a similar competition in Uruguay. It was one of the world's first international soccer tournaments. River defeated Uruguay's Bristol FC to hoist its second major trophy of the year.

# BIRTH OF A BITTER RIVALRY

The previous year, River had begun what is arguably the most significant derby in all of soccer. (In soccer, a "derby" is a game between two teams from the same city or region especially noted for the intensity of the rivalry.) In 1905, Boca Juniors had been founded in the same neighborhood as River Plate. Eight years later, it was included in a Primera División expansion. One of Boca's first games in its new division was against River. It was the first official meeting between the two clubs. (Reportedly, other games preceded the 1913 match, but no documentation exists to support such claims.) River won, 2–1. It also won two of the next four games against Boca, with the other two ending in ties. Boca finally broke through in 1918 with a 1–0 victory.

The match eventually became known as the Superclásico. *Clásico* means "classic" in Spanish, while "super" refers to the clubs' status as Argentina's most successful and popular. As Joel Richards, author of *Superclásico: Inside the Ultimate Derby*, puts it, "The rivalry in fact started as a turf war in the port area of La Boca in Buenos Aires—both were founded by the children of immigrants, both had difficulty finding land in the area for their ground, and both chose to have some

English in their name to add some perceived glamour to their club. It started out as a local rivalry before they grew to battle out who is the biggest club in the country." Sometimes the rivalry has been violent. In 1994, River defeated Boca, 2–0. Two River fans were shot and killed after the game. A Boca fan shrugged off the violence. "We tied 2–2," he smirked during a TV interview.

After a scoreless tie in 1919, the teams didn't meet for eight years. Most elite Argentine soccer teams split off in 1920 to form the Asociación Amateurs de Football (AAmF). Boca stayed behind, but River Plate joined the AAmF and won the 1920 title. The two groups continued on their separate ways until 1927, when Argentina's president, Marcelo Torcuato de Alvear, brokered an association merger. One condition was that the previous winners of both leagues would be recognized as Primera División champions. Later that year, Boca took a 1–0 victory over River as the rivalry resumed. In 1928, Boca thumped River 6–0. It remains the most one-sided game in Superclásico history.

By then, another log had been thrown on the Superclásico fire. In 1923, River moved out of La Boca to the Recoleta neighborhood, one of the most posh in Buenos Aires. So, as Richards explains, it was now "the tale of two cities, the aristocratic River Plate from the north

*Argentine president Marcelo Torcuato de Alvear helped to merge the country's football leagues.*

against the people's team, Boca Juniors, in the south." The game was well on its way to becoming what FootballDerbies.com describes as "90 minutes of deafening noise and huge avalanches of standing fans behind the goal." In 2004, the *Observer* listed the Superclásico at the top of its list of "50 Sporting Things You Must Do Before You Die." It added, "Derby day in Buenos Aires makes the Old Firm game [matching longtime Scottish rivals Celtic and Rangers] look like a primary school kick-about." By 2018, counting all 209 Primera División matches, Boca had won 76, and River had won 68. The remaining 65 games ended in ties.

Thirty years after its founding, River Plate—and Argentine soccer—was about

*In the early 1920s, River Plate moved from the poor La Boca neighborhood to the upper-class Recoleta, with its Teatro Cervantes.*

*From 1915 to 1923, the team played its games at a stadium in La Boca.*

to undergo the most important change in its history. While players had always been considered amateurs, many were paid under the table. Teams commonly offered perks such as expensive clothing and steady employment to players. This gave the players tremendous leverage. Since nothing was official, they could leave teams whenever they wanted and play elsewhere. Additionally, many European teams had already turned pro. They began making lucrative offers to South America's top players as early as 1925.

In 1931, 18 of Argentina's strongest clubs—including River and Boca—broke away to form the professional Liga Argentina de Football (LAF). As had been the case previously, both the professional and amateur groups held separate Primera División championships. The amateurs threw in the towel after the 1934 season and merged with the LAF. The combined organization was now fully professional. The former LAF

*Forward José Manuel Moreno was part of River's powerful La Máquina (The Machine) in the 1940s.*

teams all remained in the Primera División, while the others were relegated to the second level. This transition also marked the start of the Big Five. The five largest clubs in Buenos Aires—River, Boca, Racing Club, Independiente, and San Lorenzo—ruled the league. It would be 36 years before any other team won the Primera División. Even today, the Big Five continue to dominate Argentine soccer.

# El Gráfico

Winger Félix Loustau led River Plate to eight Primera División titles during the 1940s and 1950s.

# THE MILLIONAIRES AND THE MACHINE

To help cover costs, clubs had always sold memberships. There was a huge spike in membership when teams turned professional. River went from 3,661 members in 1926 to 13,686 in 1931. It had more members than any other team. It didn't waste any time spending its newfound cash, doling out 45,000 pesos (equal to nearly $1.9 million today) for 2 new players: winger Carlos Peucelle (signed in 1931 for 10,000 pesos) and forward Bernabé Ferreyra (signed in 1932 for 35,000 pesos). Because that was an immense sum of money in that era—especially with much of the world in the grip of a major economic depression—many people called River "Los Millonarios" (The Millionaires), which remains a team nickname today. Ferreyra paid immediate dividends. He tallied a league-leading 43 goals in his first season. It was the first time a River player had taken the top spot. River and Independiente tied for first in the LAF. Los Millonarios won in a playoff to claim their second Primera División title. They added two more in 1936 and another in 1937.

The original Yankee Stadium in New York City was often referred to as "The House that [Babe] Ruth Built." Team owners

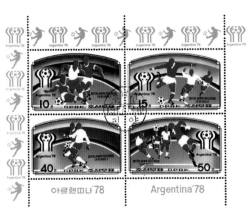

*Argentina hosted and won the World Cup in 1978.*

*River Plate jerseys have been white with a diagonal red slash consistently since the 1930s.*

felt confident that the star slugger would draw a massive increase of fans to the structure when it opened in 1923, thereby paying the construction cost. In much the same way, River goalkeeper Amadeo Carrizo said that Ferreyra's stellar play attracted many more fans than usual. Amadeo noted that the increased profits from ticket sales allowed River to build its new stadium, officially named after then club president Antonio Vespucio Liberti. Upon opening in 1938, it could accommodate up to 100,000 people, making it the country's largest stadium. It was quickly nicknamed "El Monumental." The stadium was ahead of its time in providing non-soccer facilities: a school, medical clinic, and activities for members, such as ping-pong and basketball. For forward Ángel Labruna,

Forward Alfredo "Blond Arrow" Di Stéfano was skilled at scoring.

it had another perk: he met his future wife there. In a sign of things to come, River won the inaugural game at El Monumental, defeating Peñarol of Uruguay, 3–1.

Ferreyra retired the following year. Any slack his departure created was quickly taken up by *La Máquina* (The Machine), which is still venerated as one of the best club teams of all time. With La Máquina driving the team, River won four Primera División titles from 1941 to 1947 and was runner-up twice. The "engine" consisted of five forwards: Labruna, Félix Loustau, José Manuel Moreno, Juan Carlos Muñoz, and Adolfo Pedernera. It's a tribute to their almost mythical status that this core group competed together only 18 times. Other players came in and out of the lineup, yet they are the five who remain closely associated with the nickname. It was derived from their ongoing dynamic motion, with multitalented players constantly rotating throughout the field of play. "Some go in, others come over, everyone falls back," said Peucelle, who played a key role in developing La Máquina's style of play. "Our

*River's La Máquina teams of the 1940s were some of the most dominant in South American history.*

tactical plan is not the traditional 1-2-3-5 [goalkeeper-defenders-midfielders-forwards]. It's 1-10 [goalkeeper-forwards]." Loustau acquired another nickname: "The Ventilator." He would take the ball for extended periods of time, continually changing speed and direction to confound defenders. This enabled his teammates to catch their breath before resuming their relentless attack. Perhaps the greatest compliment came from an unexpected source. Boca's Ernesto Lazatti said, "I play against La Máquina with the full intention of beating them, but as a fan of football, I would prefer to sit on the stands and watch them play."

In one respect, though, the nickname was inaccurate. A machine implies something working by rote, with each

Forward Ángel Labruna spent 20 years with River Plate, scoring 293 goals during that time.

part performing the same motion over and over. Not so, according to Labruna. "A team that has players ready for carrying out just one function can't go far," he said. La Máquina began being dismantled in 1944 when Moreno left. Pedernera departed two years later. His replacement, Alfredo Di Stéfano, would become one of soccer's all-time greats. Unfortunately for River, Di Stéfano displayed most of this greatness after he left the club.

River's domination continued beyond La Máquina's relatively brief heyday. It won five more Primera División titles between 1952 and 1957. But no one could foresee what would happen after the 1957 championship.

*Amadeo Carrizo (back center) led River Plate to its 10th Primera División title in 1952.*

# DROUGHT AND DELUGE

River failed to win a significant title for 18 years. The team wasn't bad. During that time, it finished as the runner-up 11 times in the Primera División. Sometimes it was just a point or two from the top spot. People began saying River was "five centavos short of a peso" (there are 100 centavos in a peso), meaning the team continually came close but couldn't find that little extra it needed to get to the top. During that same span, River racked up more points in the Primera División standings than any other team by scoring more goals and maintaining the second-stingiest defense.

One close call came in 1962. River and Boca were tied for first going into the

*For nearly 20 years, River failed to win a championship, despite many close calls.*

Superclásico. Boca held the lead for most of the game. With time running short, Boca keeper Antonio Roma blocked a penalty kick. That win gave Boca the league title. Four years later, River faced Peñarol in the Copa Libertadores finals. The teams split the two home games to force a third playoff match. River took a 2–0 halftime lead as Daniel Onega (who still holds a tournament-record 17 goals) scored. But River faltered in the second half, losing 4–2 as Peñarol scored twice in regulation and tacked on two more in overtime. The debacle generated yet another nickname, for losing their heads and choking in big games: "las gallinas" (the chickens). It wasn't uncommon for opposing fans to hurl dead chickens onto the pitch. A third near miss came in 1968. River, Vélez Sarsfield, and Racing Club finished in a three-way tie for first in the Primera División. Vélez won a mini-playoff to take the title.

Eventually, River fans turned the derision in their favor. Now they often sing, "Welcome to the *gallinero* [chicken coop]" as opposing teams enter El Monumental. Before this chant transpired, though, the team needed to end its drought. That finally happened in 1975 when River won both Primera División titles. One of the primary reasons was the appointment of Labruna as the team's coach. In a way, it brought the lean years full circle. The drought had begun when the team didn't renew Labruna's contract, even though he was River's all-time scoring leader.

*Daniel Onega scored 17 goals in the 1966 Copa Libertadores.*

*River Plate overcame Steaua Bucureşti in 1986 to win the Toyota Cup (as the Intercontinental was known then).*

River reached the Copa Libertadores final the following year against Brazil's Cruzeiro. The teams split the home games, which meant a third game had to be played at a neutral site. Cruzeiro had a 2–0 lead early in the second half, but River rallied to tie on a free kick and a penalty kick, both of which seemed dubious. An obvious takedown by River in the 88th minute and the resulting free kick gave the Brazilians a 3–2 victory.

The third time in the Copa Libertadores proved to be the charm for River. The team faced América de Cali of Colombia in the 1986 final. Two first-half goals gave River a 2–0 halftime edge in the first game. Despite conceding a goal moments into the second half, River hung on for a 2–1 victory. In the second match, striker Juan Gilberto Funes powered home a goal midway through the second half for the game's only tally.

Ten years later, River played in its fourth Libertadores final. The team faced its rival from the previous decade, América de Cali. The Colombians took the first game at home, 1–0. But River striker Hernán Crespo scored twice in the second game, and River won on aggregate. Then it headed for Japan to face Juventus of Italy in the Intercontinental Cup, the forerunner of the Club World Cup. Alessandro Del Piero scored the game's only goal to give the Italians the trophy. That was the high-water mark of the 1990s, which had been especially fruitful for River. It won eight Primera División titles that decade.

# MISSING OUT ON MESSI

River had an opportunity to sign future superstar Lionel Messi in 2000 when he was 12 years old. He was very impressive when he tried out for the club. But Messi suffered from a rare hormone condition that kept him from growing. His parents couldn't afford the expensive treatments, nor could local clubs. River Plate, of course, had the financial resources. But Messi lived in Rosario, about 175 miles (282 km) northwest of Buenos Aires. According to a long-established policy, River could only provide housing for players aged 13 and older. Messi's

father asked River to find him a job in Buenos Aires so the family could move there. The club refused. As Connor Parry of the blog *World Soccer Talk* explains, "One scout/coach said that if Messi didn't come, they would miss out on a great player, but others at the club said they had loads of others [recruits] just like Messi, and they would get another player just like him if he didn't sign." FC Barcelona soon stepped in and signed Messi. The rest is history.

Even though Messi was on his way across the Atlantic, the new century got off to a good start as River

*Fans suffered emotional distress when River was relegated to a lower division of play.*

continued building on the success of the 1990s. Los Millonarios won Primera División titles in 2002, 2003, and 2004. But financial troubles and mismanagement began taking a toll. In a stunning riches-to-rags story, River tumbled from first in the Primera División's Clausura tournament in 2008 to last in the Apertura tournament six months later. The bottom fell out in 2011 when River was relegated

*Striker Fernando Cavenaghi spent three different stints scoring goals for River Plate.*

for the first time in its history. The national reaction to the relegation indicated how deeply soccer is ingrained in Argentinians. Helpline centers reported a sharp increase in calls from team supporters. Psychiatrists had large numbers of River fans who wanted to be prescribed antidepressants. A lifelong fan named Enrique Cejas said, "It's the saddest day of my life, from a sporting point of view. I feel deceived by the club, by the players … not just for myself but for my children." The collective misery extended well beyond the millions of River fans. Soccer writer Horacio Pagani noted, "Argentine football has received a wound to the heart. Anyone who calls themselves a true football fan can't, sincerely, have enjoyed River Plate's relegation."

*In 2015, Marcelo Barovero and Cavenaghi helped the team to its third Copa Libertadores title.*

Fortunately for Cejas and "true football fans," River rebounded to win Primera B Nacional in 2012. Striker Fernando Cavenaghi had 19 goals to lead all scorers. River returned to the Primera División the following season. The team finished eighth in the Torneo Inicial, the season's first tournament. It improved to second in the succeeding Torneo Final. It dropped to 17th in the 2013–14 Torneo Inicial, yet it rebounded to take the top spot in the Torneo Final. An especially bright spot was Ramiro Funes Mori's late header to beat Boca Juniors at La Bombonera, Boca's home stadium. It was River's first win there in 10 years.

Later that year, River demonstrated that it had laid the demons of relegation to rest by winning the Copa Sudamericana. The team completed its transformation in 2015 by returning to the Copa Libertadores final for the first time in nearly two decades. Its opponent was the Mexican team Tigres UANL. River was fortunate to even be playing in the tournament. It had been the lowest seed among the

16 teams that qualified. And it had advanced in large part because of a gas attack by Boca fans on River players. As a result of the attack, Boca was disqualified from the tournament. But River showed that it belonged in the championship game by defeating Tigres UANL 3–0.

That victory sent them to Japan for the Club World Cup. River defeated Sanfrecce Hiroshima with forward Lucas Alario's second-half goal. It faced FC Barcelona in the final. River players and fans knew they were clearly the underdogs in the quest for a second world championship. Barcelona's 180 goals in 2015 had established a world record for goals scored in a calendar year as Messi and his teammates enjoyed one of the best-ever seasons in soccer history. Barcelona maintained its standard of excellence as it emerged with a convincing 3–0 victory.

River rebounded with a victory in the 2016 Copa Argentina, adding yet another title to the team's bulging trophy cabinet. Los Millonarios leads all other Argentine teams with 36 Primera División championships. The club also has 16 international trophies. Along with a variety of other honors, it's easy to see why River Plate is consistently regarded as one of the best soccer clubs in the world. Its millions of fans in Argentina and around the world look forward to more success in the coming years.

Lucas Alario was an efficient scorer with his right foot as well as his left.

# MEMORABLE MATCHES

## 1901

Team was founded.

## 1913
### River Plate v. Boca Juniors
*August 24, 1913, Buenos Aires, Argentina*

The first official meeting between the two towering titans of Argentine soccer was delayed for nearly an hour because the scheduled referee was a no-show. Appropriately, Irishman Paddy McCarthy came out of the stands and volunteered to officiate the game. He was a teacher who had introduced soccer to the young men who founded Boca in 1905. Cándido García's header gave River the lead midway through the first half. Antonio Ameal Pereyra extended it to 2–0 early in the second half. Boca scored at the 70-minute mark. Most contemporary chroniclers felt that Boca had the better team, but River hung on to win. The inaugural game set the tone for what would often happen in the teams' future meetings. Fistfights broke out among players during the game. Three had to leave the pitch because of injuries they sustained. Supporters of each team fought in the stands. The conflict

continued when the game was over. Riot police mounted on horseback showered gas on spectators and beat them with clubs.

# 1968

## River Plate v. Boca Juniors

*Superclásico, June 23, 1968,
Buenos Aires, Argentina*

What was otherwise an uneventful draw became infamous when the game ended. Boca fans streamed toward the exits. For some reason, the gate at Puerta (Door) 12 remained closed. In the resulting crush, 71 people were killed. Another 150 people were injured. The average age of the victims was just 19. A three-year investigation turned up several theories as to the cause. According to some accounts, fans in the upper deck threw burning flags onto fans below, sparking a stampede. Others said that River fans crossed the field and attacked Boca supporters. The gate was locked. The turnstiles wouldn't operate. Boca fans threw bags of urine at police on the field, causing them to charge into the stands to seek out the culprits. None of the explanations was ever proven. Known as the Puerta 12 tragedy, it remains the worst disaster in Argentine soccer. Since then, gates at El Monumental have been labeled with letters instead of numbers. "In Argentina, we live in a society with little memory," said Pablo Tesoriere, who made a documentary film about the event. "They changed the numbers into letters so that people don't think about la Puerta 12 or remember that 71 people died there."

# 1986

## River Plate v. FC Steaua Bucureşti

*Toyota Cup, December 14, 1986,
Tokyo, Japan*

After disappointing losses in the 1966 and 1976 Copa Libertadores finals, River finally broke through in 1986. Striker Juan Gilberto Funes and attacking midfielder Norberto Alonso scored within three minutes of each other in the first game to give River the victory. Funes scored the only goal in the second game. The victory continued Los Millonarios' run of success that year. They had already won the Primera División by a 10-point margin. Attacking midfielder Enzo Francescoli was the league's leading scorer. In Tokyo, River took on the Romanian team Steaua, the unexpected champion of the European Cup (forerunner of the Champions League), for the Toyota Cup (as the Intercontinental was known from 1980 to 2004). In the first half, River forward Antonio Alzamendi fired a shot that hit the post. The keeper couldn't control the rebound, and Alzamendi headed the ball into the net. It was the only score. Alzamendi was named Man of the Match as River notched its first world championship. "The chicken was

finally buried," said Américo Gallego, referring to opposing fans' frequent "las gallinas" taunts during the club's long championship dry spell.

# 2011

## River Plate v. Club Atlético Belgrano

### *Relegation playoff, June 26, 2011, Buenos Aires, Argentina*

River was desperately trying to avoid being relegated for the first time in its illustrious history. It had to tie or defeat Belgrano, a Primera B team, to remain in the Primera División. River dug itself into a deep crater by losing the first game 2–0. The second leg at El Monumental got off to a good start. An apparent Belgrano goal was waved off. Moments later, striker Mariano Pavone slammed the ball home to give River the lead. But Belgrano tied the score late in the game. Then Pavone missed a penalty kick. With time running out and River still down two goals, rioting fans forced an end to the game. They ripped up seats and hurled projectiles onto the field. Authorities had already deployed more than 2,200 police to the stadium and surrounding area. They employed water cannons, tear gas, batons, shields, and attack dogs, yet 35 police were injured, while 150 fans were hurt or arrested.

# 2015

## River Plate v. Boca Juniors

### *Copa Libertadores Round of 16, May 14, 2015, Buenos Aires, Argentina*

This game illustrates the depth of ill feeling between River and Boca. Boca was heavily favored to capture the cup after winning all 6 group games and outscoring opponents by 17 goals. River, on the other hand, barely squeezed into the round, winning just one group game and drawing four. Despite the odds, River won the first game at El Monumental.

The first half of the second game ended in a scoreless tie. As River players began emerging from the dressing room to start the second half, at least one Boca fan doused them with tear gas or pepper spray. Four players had to be rushed to the hospital. CONMEBOL officials called off the rest of the game. Police officers brandishing riot shields escorted the remaining River players from the field. Boca president Daniel Angelici apologized and said, "We will accept the responsibility, but I don't think the players are responsible." CONMEBOL officials decided not to replay the game. They disqualified Boca from the tournament. River was declared the winner on aggregate and eventually won the competition.

# 2015

## River Plate v. Tigres UANL

### *Copa Libertadores Finals, August 5, 2015, Buenos Aires, Argentina*

Following a scoreless tie in Mexico, the winner of the second game would be the Copa Libertadores champion. The game was extremely physical, with 44 penalties and 9 yellow cards. River took a 1–0 lead at halftime as striker Lucas Alario—who had joined the team just a few weeks earlier—scored with only a few moments remaining. Thirty minutes into the second half, River's Carlos Andrés Sánchez scored after being fouled. Ramiro Funes Mori iced the game when he converted a header off a corner kick four minutes later. "The history of this club is about fighting for these kinds of competitions," midfielder Leonardo Ponzio said. "Today is the greatest [championship] that you can achieve as a club, and we did it." The win was especially enjoyable for manager Marcelo Gallardo. He had played on River's 1996 Copa Libertadores–winning team. Having won the Copa Sudamericana eight months earlier, River held both of South America's premier club competitions. It also capped the team's turnaround from its humiliating relegation just four years earlier.

# FAMOUS FOOTBALLERS

## BERNABÉ FERREYRA

### (1909– 72)
### Forward, 1932–39

Ferreyra joined River Plate in 1932 from Club Atlético Tigre. His transfer fee, equivalent to about $1.4 million today, set a record that lasted nearly 20 years. Born in the town of Rufino, he was nicknamed "el mortero de Rufino" (the mortar of  Rufino). Ferreyra credited his brothers for his powerful strikes. He once removed his shoes to prove that he didn't have an iron bar concealed inside the toe to provide extra "oomph." On another occasion, he knocked a goalie unconscious with a booming shot. The goalie asked Ferreyra to please let him know the next time he was taking a shot so he could get out of the way. Ferreyra's style of play was physically demanding. He retired when he was just 29 years old because of the rigors his body had endured. He is one of just three players in South American soccer history to average more than a goal per game. He was so prolific that a local newspaper offered a prize to the first goalie who kept Ferreyra from scoring. Cándido De Nicola of Club Atlético Huracán eventually collected it.

## ÁNGEL LABRUNA

### (1918–83)
### Forward, 1939–59
### Manager, 1975–81

International River Fan Day is celebrated on September 28, in tribute to Ángel Labruna, whose birthday was on that date. Part of La Máquina, he ended his 20-year career as the team's all-time leading scorer (317 goals). He trailed only legendary goalkeeper Amadeo Carrizo in total games played. In 1943, he was one of three players to lead the Primera División in scoring. Two years later, he had the top spot to himself with 25 goals. In a way, Labruna was fortunate to even play professional soccer. His father often criticized him for the "wasted time" he spent playing soccer. Labruna persevered. His success wasn't limited to his playing days. The team invited him to coach, and in 1975, he guided River to its first championship in 18 years. Norberto Alonso, who played for River during Labruna's coaching years, explained that "Labruna, as a symbol of the club, knew the River style. He brought in the players that were capable of giving the extra support that the players from the academy needed to form the great team. We played with responsibility, but the focus was always on having fun."

# AMADEO CARRIZO

*(1926– )*
## Goalkeeper, 1945-68

Carrizo was one of the most revolutionary players of all time. According to the blog *A Halftime Report*, "There has been perhaps no player who has had as great an influence upon one single position as Amadeo Raúl Carrizo has had upon the position of goalkeeper." He was the first keeper to wear gloves, the first to range beyond the penalty area, and the first to employ booming kicks as a means of launching counterattacks. Sometimes Carrizo would even dribble past opposing players. His

boldness spread to his fellow keepers. As soccer writer Eduardo Galeano observed, they "refused to resign themselves to the notion that the keeper is a living wall, glued to the net. They proved he can also be a living spear." In 1968, Carrizo began wearing a cap during games. He had a clean slate for eight games, which established a record. Then a Boca player stole the cap before a match. Carrizo conceded two goals, and River Plate lost. The International Federation of Football History and Statistics (IFFHS) named him the 10th greatest goalkeeper of the 20th century. In 2013, River Plate named him the club's honorary president.

# ALFREDO DI STÉFANO

## (1926–2014)
### Forward, 1945, 1947–49
### Manager, 1981–82

Nicknamed "Saeta Rubia" (Blond Arrow), Alfredo Di Stéfano grew up in Buenos Aires and began playing for River at the age of 19. He wasn't an immediate sensation. In 1946, River loaned him to Huracán, a club in a nearby suburb. Di Stéfano returned the following year and made a lasting mark. He led the Primera División with 27 goals in 30 games as River took the championship. The combination of a player strike in 1949 and the amount of money being offered by professional Colombian teams led Di Stéfano to take his skills there. Otherwise, he might have spent his entire career with River. In 1953, he crossed the Atlantic to play for Spain's Real Madrid. There he became legendary as he helped Real win five straight Champions League titles. While Pelé is justifiably regarded as the greatest soccer player ever, Di Stéfano is generally considered the most complete all-around player. According to Football-History .net, "Di Stéfano was an incredibly versatile forward, who combined speed with a superb technique, stamina, tactical insight, and an ability to score goals."

# NORBERTO ALONSO

## (1953– )
### Attacking midfielder, 1971–76,
### 1977–81, 1984–87

Norberto "Beto" Alonso came up through River's junior team during the club's long title drought. He is often credited with anchoring the resurgence that led to two Primera División titles in 1975 and five more by 1981. Many authorities regard him as Argentina's best-ever attacking midfielder. Beto credited much of his success to his father's insistence that he play as a left-footer. "[Left-footed players] have a different attraction, are always capable of pulling something out of the hat," he said. "*Mi viejo* [my old man] made me left-footed. I would stand still on my right foot, wait for a ball he'd send, and hit a volley using my left foot." He even out-Peléd Pelé in 1972, scoring what became known as a "dummy goal." A teammate passed the ball downfield. As the goalie bent down to scoop up the ball, Beto raced right in front of him. The distracted goalie let the ball roll past him. Beto circled behind the goalie and shot at the now-open goal. Pelé had tried the same maneuver in the 1970 World Cup. He missed. Beto didn't—he scored. With his left foot, of course.

# DANIEL PASSARELLA

**(1953– )**
**Defender, 1974-82, 1988-89**
**Manager, 1989-94, 2006-07**
**President, 2009-13**

Daniel Passarella is widely considered one of South America's best-ever defenders. He did more than help protect the goal. He often moved forward to join the attack. His 134 goals in 451 matches was a record for a defender for many years. Though he stood just 5-foot-8, he was noted for his ability to elevate and was always a threat to head in corner kicks. He was known as "El Gran Capitán" (The Great Captain). Another nickname was "El Kaiser" (The Emperor), in honor of Franz Beckenbauer of Germany, one of the most dominant players in the 1960s and '70s. The nicknames reflected his on-field leadership. Substantiating Passarella's physical style of play, the *London Times* ranked him 36th on its 2007 list of the "50 Hardest Footballers," in part due to his

elbow jabs when the referee's attention was elsewhere. "Looked every inch the Latin American desperado from central casting, and tackled with the ferocity of the wild bull of the Pampas," said the citation. Passarella was elected the club's president in 2009.

# RIVER PLATE TITLES
## THROUGH 2017

**INTERCONTINENTAL CUP**

1986
Total: 1

**SUPERCOPA SUDAMERICANA**

1997
Total: 1

**COPA SUDAMERICANA**

2014
Total: 1

**COPA LIBERTADORES**

Winner
1986
1996
2015
Total: 3

Runner-up
1966
1976
Total: 2

**RECOPA SUDAMERICANA**

2015
2016
Total: 2

**COPA ARGENTINA**

2016
Total: 1

**PRIMERA DIVISIÓN/ SUPERLIGA**

1920
1932
1936 (2)
1937
1941
1942
1945
1947
1952
1953
1955
1956
1957
1975 (2)
1977
1979 (2)
1980
1981
1986
1990
1991
1993
1994
1996
1997 (2)
1999
2000
2002
2003
2004
2008
2014
Total: 36

# SELECTED BIBLIOGRAPHY

Dempsey, Luke. *Club Soccer 101: The Essential Guide to the Stars, Stats, and Stories of 101 of the Greatest Teams in the World.* New York: W. W. Norton, 2014.

Galeano, Eduardo. *Soccer in Sun and Shadow.* Translated by Mark Fried. New York: Nation Books, 2013.

Goldblatt, David, and Johnny Acton. *The Soccer Book: The Sport, the Teams, the Tactics, the Cups.* 3rd ed. New York: DK, 2014.

Mason, Tony. *Passion of the People?: Football in South America.* New York: Verso, 1995.

Richards, Joel. *Superclásico: Inside the Ultimate Derby.* Kindle edition. Seattle, Wash.: BackPage Press, 2013.

Wilson, Jonathan. *Angels with Dirty Faces: How Argentinian Soccer Defined a Nation and Changed the Game Forever.* New York: Nation Books, 2016.

# WEBSITES

## OFFICIAL SITE OF THE ARGENTINE FOOTBALL ASSOCIATION

*http://www.afa.org.ar/*

The official AFA website previews upcoming games, notes the results and statistics of past matches, and highlights league news.

## RIVER PLATE

*http://www.cariverplate.com.ar/en*

The official website of Club Atlético River Plate includes information regarding matches, club news, team history, titles, and more.

Note: Every effort has been made to ensure that the websites listed above are suitable for children, that they have educational value, and that they contain no inappropriate material. However, because of the nature of the Internet, it is impossible to guarantee that these sites will remain active indefinitely or that their contents will not be altered.

# INDEX